What's Your
FRO-blem?

De-Ann Smith

Clovercroft Publishing

Published by Clovercroft Publishing, Franklin, Tennessee

Published in association with Larry Carpenter of Christian Book Services, LLC
www.christianbookservices.com

Cover design by Naomi Gibson

Cover and Interior Illustrations by Naomi Gibson

Interior Design by Suzanne Lawing

Printed in the United States of America

978-1-954437-18-0

Dedication

To all black boys and girls across the world, this is for you!

For parents who want to teach their children to value
who they are naturally, this is for you!

For those of a different race, culture or ethnicity open to learning or
teaching their children about embracing differences, this is for you.

This is for all who have been told or have grown to believe the way
their hair naturally grows out of their heads isn't beautiful.

Black kings and queens, this is for us!

Big and bouncy,

Curly and springy
Short, long
My hair is my crown

My hair is neat

My hair smells sweet

What's your **FRO-blem?**

My hair is awesome

My edges are **flawless**
A true natural goddess
"It's perfect, mummy promise!"
"Daddy's little princess"

This is how my hair grows

This is how God made me

What's your **FRO-blem?**

I'm handsome and happy

I'm **strong** like my hair
I bounce everywhere
I love all its waves
It helps me feel

brave

My bun is cute!

My braids are nice!

What's your **FRO-blem?**

My future is
bright!

Wash day and detangle
Squared parts and triangles

Corkscrew or Bantu
Check out my hairdo

Afro-pick pulling plaits
Spiky, sponged curls
What's your **FRO-blem?**
Look how it swirls

Twistout and blowout
Cornrows and locs

Look at my braids
I rock it with shades

Sleep with my **bonnet**

That's how I keep it

Puffy
puff
puff

I like how it fluffs
I love all its kinks
Even when it shrinks

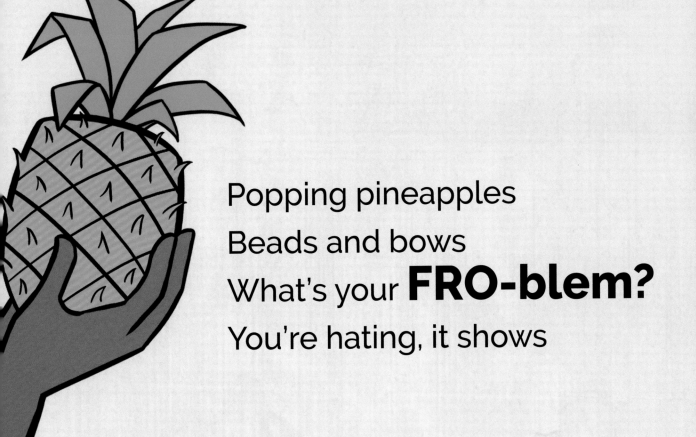

Popping pineapples
Beads and bows
What's your **FRO-blem?**
You're hating, it shows

Spin, spin

in the barber's chair

Stay still when he cuts my hair

Low cut with a lineup

I love a sharp look

Fresh fade and high-top

Stepping out clean

What's Your **FRO-blem?**

Confidence is key

My hair is **royal**
A precious jewel

Covered in satin
Smooth like my skin

Big smile on my face

My hair I embrace

Loving my skin

All of its **melanin**

Crush goals, reach the sky
Never give up, try and try
FRO team, we're smart and kind
Creative, with positive minds

Like our hair, we're so unique

The way we **dance**,

to the way we speak

No matter what, we will achieve

All of our **dreams**,

if we believe

Cute coily coils
Scented hair oils

What's your **FRO-blem?**

Do you have a problem?

Acknowledgements

This journey started long before I decided to finally publish this book. This was sitting on my laptop for a few years. I must say thank you to everyone who decided to come along for the ride in their own unique way. Each of you have played a part and you know how.

My support system extends even beyond the names listed but I'm thankful to the below mentioned, specifically, for their contribution to the What's Your FRO-blem journey!

Thanks to my illustrator Naomi Gibson for bringing my dream to life. You nailed it!

I'm forever grateful to my amazing mother Rachel Sanderson. You are my rock!

Thanks to the rest of my family: Ro-Ann, Kerri-Ann, JD, Jaden and Kenai Smith; Joy-Ann, Markland and Jhai O'Connor and Alana Alleyne. You were all rooting for me!

Friends: Kerisha Went, Kanesha Arthur, Kevon Delaney, Melissa Taylor, Claire Griffith, Talicia Welcome, Jason Waterman, Ammuniki Wood and Keila Bradshaw.

My mentor Janelle "Jaycee" Mayers love ya!

Special mention to these beautiful, intelligent children: McKenzie Mayers, Keniyah Bradshaw, Azaria Taylor, Summer-Rayn Gittens, Cynara Devonish and Rajae McCollin. Thanks for your contributions!

I'm forever grateful to God for this journey.

Thank you to all who will support this book.

About the Author

De-Ann Smith, affectionately called Dee, found her passion for writing from early teenage years. This Barbadian writer has her master's degree in Creative Writing from Northumbria University in Newcastle, United Kingdom and a bachelor's degree in Mass Communications (Journalism) from Winston-Salem State University, North Carolina, USA.

Dee also attended Sheridan College, Wyoming, USA, as well as The Alexandra School, Barbados and Barbados Community College where she took her first creative writing class and loved it.

Dee is a blogger and she owns a natural hair and skin products line. Professionally, she is a Digital Marketer who uses her passion of writing daily.

Apart from writing, Dee loves family and volleyball. She is a former scholarship, semi pro and national volleyball athlete as well as a former junior national assistant coach.

About the Illustrator

Naomi "Afrohdita" Gibson is a Barbadian mixed media artist based in the United Kingdom. She studied Visual Arts at Barbados Community College and is currently completing a bachelor's degree in Graphic Design (Visual Communication and Illustration) at the University of West London, United Kingdom.

She is also an alum of The Alexandra School, Barbados.

Afrohdita enjoys working with pen and ink, and is interested in experimenting with different line weights and textures to create a drawing/piece. Influenced by other creatives and sunny and rainy days, she loves music with a funky base line. Afrohdita is also inspired by animation especially cartoons and anime from childhood to present day.

More Information

Facebook: @DeeSaysSo

Instagram: @DeeSaysSo

Twitter: @DeeSaysSoBlog

Email: deesaysso@gmail.com

Website: DeeSaysSo.com